TED
KENNEDY

Library of Congress Number: 79-27299

1 2 3 4 5 6 7 8 9 0 84 83 82 81 80

Printed in the United States of America.

Library of Congress Cataloging in Publication Data

Aschburner, Steve.
  Ted Kennedy, the politician and the man.

  SUMMARY: A biography of Ted Kennedy discussing
both his political and personal life.
  1. Kennedy, Edward Moore, 1932-   — Juvenile
literature. 2. Legislators — United States — Biography — Juvenile literature. 3. United States.
Congress. Senate — Biography — Juvenile literature.
[1. Kennedy, Edward Moore, 1932-   2. Legisla-
tors] I. Title.
E840.8.K35A82   973.92'092'4 [B][92]   79-27299
ISBN 0-8172-0430-X

PHOTO CREDITS
Page 5, Gamma/Liaison; 7, (top left) UPI, (top right) UPI,
(bottom) Wide World Photos; 8, Dennis Brack, Black Star; 13, UPI;
15, UPI; 18, Wide World Photos; 22, Wide World Photos; 25, (top left)
UPI; (top right) Wide World Photos; (bottom) UPI; 27, Wide World Photos;
31, Wide World Photos; 32, Wide World Photos; 35, Wide World Photos;
36, (top left) Charles Bonnay, Black Star; (top right) UPI; (bottom)
Robert Lackenbach, Black Star; 39, Wide World Photos; 43, Jack Hubbard,
Black Star; 45, Dennis Brack, Black Star

The Politician and ★★★★ the Man ★★★★

TED KENNEDY

by Steve Aschburner

RAINTREE PUBLISHERS

Milwaukee • Toronto • Melbourne • London

★★★★★★ 1 ★★★★★★

THE DECISION

On November 7, 1979, Senator Edward M. Kennedy of Massachusetts stood in historic Faneuil Hall in Boston. He fidgeted with his necktie, cleared his throat, and said:

"I take the course compelled by events and by my commitment to public life. Today, I formally announce that I am a candidate for President of the United States."

A large crowd of Kennedy supporters cheered loudly, almost drowning out the rest of the speech.

But the important words had been said. It was now official. One year to the day before the 1980 election, Edward Kennedy had said that he would seek the Democratic Presidential nomination. He would try to do what no one had done in this century — snatch the nomination away from a President of his own party, President Jimmy Carter.

And yet, for all the excitement, no one was really surprised.

From Edward Kennedy's youngest days — when he was just starting to be called by his nickname

A bust of John Adams seems to look on as another Massachusetts man runs for President.

"Ted" — everyone assumed that some day he would have an important place in the United States government. His brother John Fitzgerald Kennedy became a Congressman, a Senator, and in 1960, the thirty-fifth President. Another brother, Robert Francis Kennedy, was U.S. Attorney General, a Senator, and in 1968, a candidate for the Presidency.

So for Ted, it was not a question of what or why. It was just a question of when.

The Kennedy family has always held a special place in the hearts of the American people. They were young, rich, good-looking, and most of all powerful. Led by John Kennedy, they came into America's public life at a time when there was a great hope for the future.

When John F. Kennedy was elected President there was no war. It was a time of plenty. People had a faith that politics, and the right leaders, could make their lives even better. And a great deal of this faith was given to the Kennedys.

The family came to be treated almost as the royal family of the United States. In fact, like royalty, they seemed to offer a dynasty to the American people. As the Chicago Tribune suggested after John Kennedy was elected President, "President John Kennedy, 1961-1969; President Robert Kennedy, 1969-1977; President Edward Kennedy, 1977-1985. . . ."

Robert Kennedy discusses politics with his young brother.

The inauguration of John F. Kennedy, 1961.

The President and his younger brothers in 1962.

Ted, with Joan and his three children, stands at his brother's grave.

So when John Kennedy was assassinated in Dallas, Texas in 1963, Robert Kennedy became the logical choice to follow him as President. And when Robert Kennedy was assassinated in Los Angeles, California, in 1968, Ted Kennedy, the last of the Kennedy brothers, became the "heir apparent."

But just being their brother could not be reason enough. When a baseball player is injured, for example, the manager doesn't give the player's brother a uniform and expect him to do the same things his brother did. Then why should a man become President just because his brother held the job?

Perhaps the American people wanted another Kennedy in the White House because they would like to relive the good memories of the earlier Kennedy.

Also, John and Robert Kennedy were plucked away from the American people before the people were ready. The Kennedys never had the chance to do all they might have done. Putting Ted Kennedy into the White House might keep the promise that had been broken by two bullets.

So John Kennedy may have known more than most people when he handed Ted a small gift on the day of John's inauguration in January, 1961. Ted unwrapped the gift to find a small, silver cigarette box. Engraved on the box were the words from the Bible, "And the last shall be first."

FAMILY AND CHILDHOOD

Joseph and Rose Kennedy had nine children between the years 1915 and 1932: Joseph Jr., John, Rosemary, Kathleen, Patricia, Eunice, Robert, Jean and Edward. The youngest, Edward, was born on February 22, 1932. It was a great date in American history, the two-hundredth anniversary of the birth of George Washington.

But unlike George Washington, or Abraham Lincoln, or many other great American leaders, Edward Kennedy had a head start. His was no rags-to-riches story.

It is true that Ted's ancestors were Irish farmers in southeastern Ireland. His great-grandfather, Patrick J. Kennedy, left Ireland during the great potato famine of the 1840s and settled in Boston.

But Ted's grandfather P. J. Kennedy worked hard, and became a saloon keeper, realtor and banker. His mother's father, John F. Fitzgerald, was a colorful and successful politician. Nicknamed "Honey Fitz" for the favors he did his friends, he served in the state

Senate, the U.S. House of Representatives, and was mayor of Boston for three terms.

Ted's father Joseph was also a self-made millionaire. He was involved in banking, the stock market, liquor wholesaling, real estate, and motion picture production. By the time Ted was born in 1932, Joe Kennedy had built a fortune estimated at 250 million dollars.

So the house in Hyannis Port, Massachusetts, where Ted Kennedy first lived, was not a log cabin.

Teddy was influenced by many people during his growing years. When grandfather Honey Fitz was 75 years old, he would grab Ted's pudgy, six-year-old hand and take him on long walks around Boston. These walks, and the love Ted felt for his grandfather, also became a love for Boston.

The Kennedy youngsters helped raise each other, too. Joe Jr., 15 years older than Ted, was more than a big brother to him. He was looked up to, like a family idol. John, Bobby and the girls also helped raise young Ted.

His parents certainly loved him, and as the youngest and last of the Kennedys, Ted may have been their favorite. But, as Rose said many years later, "You wonder if the mother and father aren't quite tired when the ninth one comes along . . . There were 17 years between my oldest and youngest child, and I had been telling bedtime stories for 20 years."

So, there may have been some distance between Ted and his parents. Mr. Kennedy was a harsh father, sometimes treating his children as if they were business partners instead of kids. He demanded serious discussion at the dinner table. And he was often absent, away from home on business. That left Mrs. Kennedy to quiz the children on current events and make them read a selected book one hour each day.

Mr. Kennedy loved his children and wanted them to have fun. But he made one thing clear to them: Just because they were wealthy, just because they had a head start on other youngsters, that didn't mean they could be lazy. In fact, they were expected to work all that much harder, since they had advantages that other families did not.

Ted received an allowance of just 10¢ per week when he was little and only 25¢ later on. He delivered newspapers, cut neighbors' lawns, and cleaned the bridle path for his father.

Mr. Kennedy expected one other thing of his children: He wanted them to succeed, more than anything else. What a fellow did with his life was not as important as winning at whatever he chose. The Kennedy youngsters were taught to compete — and to win.

In the early days, this showed in the Kennedy

Bobby and Ted on their first day of school in England.

children's sports. They played all sports together, from touch football to tennis to baseball. And Teddy was the "perfect kid brother." Chubby and cheerful, he would gladly run errands for the older youngsters. He would catch fly balls, run into the bushes to retrieve footballs, and tie up the boat for his brothers.

The Kennedys moved many times during Teddy's childhood, to bigger and better houses as Mr. Kennedy's family — and fortune — grew. The biggest move of all came in 1938, when Ted was just six years old. Joe Kennedy had been appointed by President Franklin D. Roosevelt as American ambassador to England. Joe Jr., and John were away at college by now, but the rest of the family moved into a huge, 36-room mansion in London. They had 23 servants, 3 chauffeurs and a fleet of cars. Teddy and brother Bobby became playmates of Princesses Elizabeth and Margaret of England.

But there were some disadvantages. England was a land in trouble at the time, for World War II was just around the corner. Teddy and Bobby would watch men and women running in the streets, digging trenches and preparing for war. And between kindergarten and college, Ted attended 10 different schools in 10 different places.

After returning to the U.S. in 1939, the family spent its summers at Hyannis Port, and winters in

Teddy stands in front of the new Ambassador to England and some of his family.

Palm Beach, Florida. Many of the schools Ted was shuffled in and out of were private. This meant that he would live away from home and only be with his family on weekends. But that's how the parents wanted it. They were busy.

When Ted was eight years old, he was put into the seventh grade with Bobby. He immediately had trouble getting along. The older boys picked on him, laughed at him and beat him up. But the seventh grade tests hurt even more.

Ted switched to a new school three months later,

and his grades began to improve. He became president of his seventh grade and played on a basketball team. His best subjects were geography, French and arithmetic. His worst was spelling. His grades were mostly Bs and Cs. Nothing special.

Not yet.

★ ★ ★ ★ ★ ★ 3 ★ ★ ★ ★ ★ ★
SCHOOL

The Kennedy men had always been good at sports. Joe Sr., Joe Jr., John and Bobby had all played football. And Ted, rapidly growing towards his 6-foot 2-inches and 205 pounds, seemed to have the perfect build for the sport.

So life seemed almost like a paradise when he enrolled in Milton Academy, a private boarding school a few miles south of Boston.

Bobby had liked Milton, and soon so did Ted. It became his second home. He was active in sports, participating in the intramural wrestling and basketball teams and playing on the varsity tennis team.

But football was his first love, and he played left end on the varsity for two years. He seemed to love the shock of physical contact. And his exuberance showed through off the football field as well, for teachers and classmates remembered him as cheerful and charming. In fact, he was called "Smilin' Ed" by some friends.

The only time Ted wasn't smiling was when it was

The determined young football player from Harvard.

time to do his schoolwork. The years of switching from school to school, piecing together his education, began to catch up with him. Though he was good at debate (a skill that would come in handy later in life), he needed the help of many tutors to make it through his four years at Milton. Again, he was a B and C student, with few outstanding qualities at that point besides his nice personality.

Of course, he didn't need many. It was 1950, time for college, and Ted was going to Harvard, where his father and brothers had gone.

Ted fit easily into the world of Harvard, the prestigious school near Boston. Here he was surrounded by the sons of great men, and being the son of Joseph Kennedy was not too impressive. It helped Ted to attract little attention, while he put his mind to other things.

His schoolwork was one of those things. Sports, girls and parties were others. Ted was assigned to Winthrop House on campus, where most of the athletes lived. They were an even more fun-loving group than Ted, so he became known as a hard worker in this group. He would not drop his studies as others would to run off for fun. He would yell out "Hold it down!" if he was trying to read.

But sometimes he couldn't work hard enough. Spanish was an especially difficult class for Ted, and he was told that if he didn't improve his C-minus grade, he might be kicked off the football team. Ted became almost sick with the worry of losing the sport he loved most.

His athlete friends were ready to help, however, and Ted agreed to let one of them, who was very good in Spanish, take the final exam in his place.

The professor found out. He recognized the other student. The cheating was reported and both were expelled, with the condition that they would be readmitted in a year if they were good citizens.

The cheating incident was discussed years later when Ted ran for political office. But it did not seem to hurt his reputation. Many people dismissed it as a college-boy prank, and administrators from Harvard even praised Ted for "taking his medicine like a man."

Looking back, Ted admitted that he had made a bad mistake. "What I did was wrong," he said. "I have regretted it ever since."

Ted was embarrassed and ashamed, but most of all he was afraid of what his father would say. Mr. Kennedy had always stressed competition and winning, but he didn't want his sons to cheat to get there. When Ted told his father of the incident, his father listened to every detail. The next day he exploded in anger.

The only choice, as Ted saw it, was to join the

service. His brothers had both been in the Navy. Maybe, Ted thought, by going away to serve his country he could save his family from some disgrace. So he signed up for the Army.

His two years were unexciting, but safe. He spent time in France and Germany. He suffered through basic training, but said years later that it helped him mature. He did not find glory in the Army, but he came out more grown-up.

By the time Ted returned to Harvard in 1953, he was the brother of a United States Senator, John. More seemed to be expected of him now, and Ted responded to the challenge. He got an A in Spanish to put to rest the old memories, and his other grades improved as he worked harder. He served as a volunteer basketball coach for underprivileged youngsters. He worked hard at football, too, and made the varsity.

In the spring of 1956, Ted graduated from Harvard. He had worked hard, and majored in government. His best work was in public speaking. Again, his grades were slightly better than average and he graduated in the top half of his class — barely.

Because his grades were merely fair, Harvard's Law School turned Ted down. Ted didn't seem to mind much, however, because he wanted to move to California to attend Stanford University. But Joe

Senator John F. Kennedy talks to his brother during Ted's graduation from Harvard.

Kennedy decided that Ted would enroll that autumn in the University of Virginia Law School.

Ted was a different student at the University of Virginia. Though his grades were again average, he worked long and hard hours. He felt he had to.

"I've got to go at a thing four times as hard and four times as long as some other fellow," he said. "I had to, just to keep up with some of the other guys."

In June of 1959, Ted graduated with his law degree. Politics seemed a likely choice for him and his record was good enough. But he didn't know yet what direction he was headed in.

Perhaps he didn't need to know. His brothers would point the way.

★ ★ ★ ★ ★ ★ ★ 4 ★ ★ ★ ★ ★ ★ ★
NEW BEGINNINGS

Ted Kennedy looked especially handsome as he stood at the lectern, speaking for the family at dedication ceremonies for the Kennedy Physical Education building at Manhattanville College. He was a sophomore in law school in the fall of 1957, and he enjoyed the chance to sharpen up his public speaking skills. Even if it did mean wearing a suit and tie.

Ted's sister Jean was also there, with her parents and sister Eunice. While a student at Manhattanville, Jean roomed with Ethel Sakel. She had introduced Ethel to her brother Bobby and the two eventually married. Now she was about to do the same to Ted. Jean ran into Joan Bennett, a pretty, blonde student. She introduced Joan to Ted.

Ted and Joan spent the rest of that day, and many other days, together. They talked on the phone constantly, and Ted visited whenever he could.

Ted had dated many girls before Joan Bennett, but he apparently had found what he had been looking for. In the spring of 1958 Ted Kennedy asked Mr. Harry Bennett for permission to marry his daughter.

Cardinal Spellman marries Ted and Joan.

Ted (left), John (center), and Robert (right), at a formal dinner in 1958.

Joan and Ted pose for reporters, with Senator John Kennedy behind them.

Mr. Bennett, an advertising executive, grinned and asked, "Do you think you could support my daughter in the style to which she has been accustomed?"

About 475 guests watched as Ted Kennedy and Joan Bennett were married on November 29, 1958 in a small church in Bronxville, New York. Bobby was the chief usher and John was the best man. At the reception, the brothers had to be dragged from a tavern where they were watching the Army-Navy football game. Joan Bennett Kennedy learned quickly that this was no ordinary family she had married into.

Their honeymoon in Nassau lasted just three days. After that, Ted had to be back in law classes at Virginia.

Late that October, a major meeting was held at Bobby's Hyannis Port home. The Kennedy brothers had invited a group of close advisers also. They decided that John would run for the Democratic presidential nomination. Bobby would be the campaign manager, and young Ted, fresh from law school, would be responsible for getting support from 11 Western states.

Now, Ted had gained a little political experience in 1958 as the manager of John's Senate campaign. But John's victory then was almost assured, and other men did a lot of the work. Ted mostly shook hands and watched.

John and Ted return from a sail during John's 1960 presidential campaign.

The campaign of 1960 was to be different. Although the Kennedys, a city family, did not have much appeal out West, a presidential candidate needs all the support he can get. It was Ted's job to deliver the support.

Ted plunged in head first. He searched for support in the mountains, in the desert, in the farmlands. He did whatever was necessary to win over the crowds — bronc-busting at rodeos, ski-jumping at Colorado resorts, landing a plane with only a little training. He worked hard at the difficult job.

It was difficult for Joan, too. The young couple was apart for weeks at a time. Ted returned to Bronxville for the birth of his daughter Kara Anne on February 27, but a month later was back on the campaign trail. This time, Joan, who had no interest in politics before, was at his side.

They were rewarded in Los Angeles on June 13, 1960. John Kennedy needed just 11 more delegate votes to gain the Democratic nomination. It was Wyoming's turn to vote, one of Ted's assigned states. The youngest brother was already smiling widely on the convention floor when Wyoming cast all 15 of its votes for John F. Kennedy.

It was Ted's first political success. It would not be his last.

★ ★ ★ ★ ★ ★ ★ 5 ★ ★ ★ ★ ★ ★ ★

THE YOUNG POLITICIAN

Ted Kennedy had helped John become President. Now it was John's turn to help Ted.

Their father Joe Kennedy had seen a son enter the White House. Another son, Bobby, was going to hold the nation's fourth most powerful position, Attorney General. He was happy about that, but he wanted more.

"You boys have what you want and everybody worked to help you get it," he told John and Bobby in 1961. "Now it's Teddy's turn."

What Ted wanted was a position in the United States Senate. He had been pointed in that direction ever since his graduation from law school, and in his heart he felt he was ready.

The only problem was that, according to his age, he wasn't ready. The Constitution requires Senators to be at least 30 years old, and Ted, who was working as an assistant district attorney in Boston, was just 29.

However, John Kennedy's Senate seat had been empty since his election. The governor of Massachusetts appointed Benjamin Smith to fill the position. Smith was a friend of the Kennedys. After his two-year term, he stepped down so Ted could run for the seat.

During the Christmas season of 1961, Joe Kennedy suffered a stroke. It left him paralyzed and unable to talk. That illness gave Ted another reason for running for the Senate. He wanted to show his sick father that he could win.

There was a great deal of criticism of Ted's decision to run for the Senate. Even Ted himself admitted that his past record contained little to show he could do the job. Many critics said that, if his name had been anything but Kennedy, he would never have had a chance.

Even some Kennedy supporters were worried. They felt that other politicians would be offended that Ted started his career so near the top.

But the Kennedys gambled. They didn't listen to the critics. They trusted the public.

Led by brother-in-law Stephen Smith, Ted set up a campaign. Like John's two years earlier, it stressed Ted's personal appeal and his freshness. And it worked. Within seven months, Ted Kennedy had defeated fellow Democrat Ed McCormack and Republican George Lodge. He was now the junior Senator from the state of Massachusetts. He could join his brothers in Washington, D.C.

The Boston crowd reaches out to Ted during his Senate campaign.

Ted accepts the Democratic nomination for Senator.

Ted knew that many eyes would be upon him in his early days as a Senator. Many people wanted to see him fail. Others wanted to see him act cocky and offend the veteran Senators.

But because Ted was aware of all this, none of it happened. He came to Washington at the peak of his brother's popularity. He didn't challenge the power structure of the Senate. He worked on services for his home state.

"Freshmen should be seen and not heard," he said. Ted tried his power on for size, but was cautious. He was an ideal, if careful, new Senator. No wonder that brother John called him "the best politician of us all."

In fact, Ted was performing one of a freshman Senator's duties, presiding over the Senate, on November 22, 1963. A Senate aide rushed through the chamber doors and interrupted the day's proceedings. He brought news, bad news, and it moved like the ripples of a wave across the floor. Finally the aide ran up to Ted.

"Senator Kennedy," the aide said. "Your brother the President has been shot!"

★★★★★★ 6 ★★★★★★
HARD TIMES

It has been said that people learn and grow by living through tragedies. If that is the case, Ted Kennedy learned more and grew bigger than almost anyone in America in the 1960s.

As of November 22, 1963, Bobby was the head of the Kennedy family. But Ted too gained great responsibility. It was Ted who told his mother Rose of the tragedy in Dallas, Texas. It was Ted who broke the terrible news to his father Joe, who was already dangerously sick.

Ted, like all the Kennedys, felt a deep, personal grief. But he showed his sorrow by working harder. Hard work allowed him to take out his frustrations, his anger and his sadness.

And the work was becoming harder all the time. Just as there was a void left in the hearts of the American people after John Kennedy's death, there was also a void left in Ted's political life.

Lyndon Johnson was now President of the United States. Johnson, Vice-President under John Kennedy,

Ted and Joseph Kennedy in 1964.

was a different man from the Kennedys. Yet Johnson saw Ted Kennedy, the quiet young Senator, as a friend. Only now, Kennedy was not so polite or quiet. He had gained some experience and confidence.

Ted's first Senate speech was a bold one. It was on the Civil Rights Bill, designed to fight discrimination

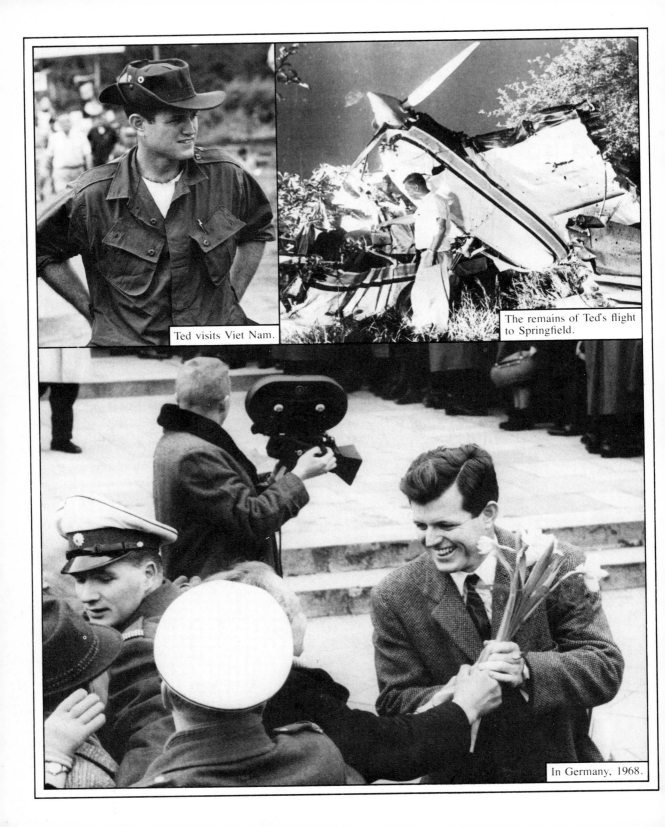

Ted visits Viet Nam.

The remains of Ted's flight to Springfield.

In Germany, 1968.

against black people. He felt a need to act, to do more than just watch and listen. And he may have realized that time can run out, as it did for his brother John.

Time almost ran out for Ted Kennedy on June 19, 1964. Leaving the Senate late, he took a small plane to a political rally in Springfield, Massachusetts. When the pilot tried to land in the fog, the plane crashed. The pilot and another man died. Ted Kennedy was thrown against the ceiling and lay motionless. His back was broken.

In 1944, Ted's oldest brother Joe Jr. had been killed when his World War II plane was shot down. In 1948, Ted's older sister Kathleen was killed in a plane crash. Now, in 1964, Ted Kennedy had suffered a plane crash. Bobby explained it the only way he knew how: "I guess the only reason we've survived is that there are too many of us. There are more of us than there is trouble."

Ted was in serious condition for a while. If the back injury had been an inch higher, he would have been paralyzed for life. But when Ted learned that he would regain the use of his legs, he was determined to walk again by Christmas.

However, 1964 was an election year, and Ted ran his campaign from a hospital bed. He was strapped into a heavy metal brace for months. Joan did his legwork and went to many of the functions in her husband's place. And when the votes were counted that fall, Ted Kennedy had won his position by the largest majority in the history of the state. Bobby, who had resigned as Attorney General, won a Senate seat from New York.

The brothers went back to Washington a more serious pair. They worked long and hard for the Civil Rights Act of 1965, which was designed to get rid of poll taxes. Poll taxes were paid by people wanting to vote; thus, poor people couldn't pay the taxes and couldn't vote. The Kennedys saw this as unfair. Finally, in 1966, the United States Supreme Court agreed with them.

Ted visited Viet Nam in 1965 and saw the horrors of the war there. Though the first Kennedy administration may have caused much of the war, Ted and Bobby were slowly becoming opposed to it, Bobby even more than Ted.

The two brothers were also becoming closer to each other. They would take long walks together, and give each other political and mental support.

Bobby especially needed Ted's support in 1968, when he decided to run for the Democratic nomination for President. Ted was in charge of putting together an instant campaign for his brother. Together, they started their run for the nomination.

The primary election in California was important to the campaign and Ted went to San Francisco to take charge of the northern half of the state. Bobby stayed in Los Angeles for the southern half. Things went well and victory seemed just around the corner.

Ted had just returned from a victory rally and switched on his television set in the hotel room to watch the celebration in Los Angeles. Instead, he saw an uproar.

Standing in the middle of the room, staring at the set, Ted Kennedy realized that Robert Kennedy had been shot.

Ted gives the eulogy at Robert's funeral.

★★★★★★ 7 ★★★★★★
YEARS IN THE SENATE

Time passed in sadness for Ted Kennedy. Thirteen months after Bobby Kennedy was killed by assassin Sirhan Sirhan, Richard Nixon, a Republican, was in the White House. Ted Kennedy had fought off a "Draft Kennedy" movement for President at the Democratic convention. It had risen up out of the sympathy for the last Kennedy brother.

Ted himself was very depressed. As he did after John's death, he buried himself in work. But it was not enough. He would disappear on his sailboat or take long walks alone on the beach. He felt responsible for 12 fatherless nieces and nephews.

Maybe the party on Chappaquiddick Island on July 18, 1969, was an effort to forget those bad times. If it was, it failed. It was meant to be a cookout for some women who had worked for Bobby's campaign. It was held outdoors at a cottage on a tiny chunk of land near Martha's Vineyard. The six women were joined by six men, including Ted Kennedy and his cousin Joe Gargan.

First food and drinks were brought to the cottage. Then came the guests. All the trips took time, because the island was separated from the mainland by a 500-foot wide channel that was crossed by a small ferry boat.

A little after 11 p.m., Ted Kennedy was talking with Mary Jo Kopechne, a 28-year-old loyal worker for Bobby. He glanced at his watch and said he wanted to return to town. Mary Jo also said she was tired and wanted to leave.

The two left in Kennedy's car, and drove a half-mile. The Kennedy car reached an unrailed, wooden bridge, but toppled over the side into the darkness. It turned upside down, with the roof resting under ten feet of water.

Ted Kennedy said later that he thought he would drown, but then found himself coming to the surface. He said he dove several times to rescue Mary Jo but could not find her.

After he regained his strength, Kennedy walked back to the cottage. Two friends went with him and also tried to help, he said. They too failed.

Kennedy swam across the channel to his hotel room, and reported the accident the following morning. Sometime after 10 a.m., Mary Jo's body was removed from the car.

Kennedy issued a sworn statement after the

accident, but not everyone believed him. Rumors and questions swirled about. The details seemed to become less clear with time.

The critics saw the accident, and Kennedy's action after it, as a sign that he could not be trusted. They feared that the pressures of the Presidency would be too great for such a man. They called it a "character flaw."

But other people saw it almost as a character builder. Ted Kennedy was no longer the carefree, lucky, rich boy. He no longer took things for granted. They said that now, Ted Kennedy knew what it was to suffer.

The suffering did not end there. Joe Kennedy died later in 1969. Illness plagued his family and Teddy, Jr., lost a leg in a cancer operation in 1973.

And Ted Kennedy again responded as Kennedys had in the past. He lost himself in his work in the Senate. He became one of the most respected and powerful Senators in Congress.

He also became one of the hardest working Senators. He and his staff would work from early in the mornings until late at night on important issues. He learned how to fight for his goals in congress and he made friends with powerful businessmen. He did anything he could to accomplish what he felt was important.

Ted faces reporters after the Chappaquidick incident.

"What I'm trying to do is serve, hopefully, as a voice for the powerless . . . [the] people left out of the system," Senator Kennedy said. The man who had so much and such a head start on everyone else had not forgotten that others were not so fortunate.

"If you can't read the Bill of Rights, it doesn't do you very much good, does it? All those words in the Constitution — if you're too sick, you can't have freedom of religion, because you can't get to church. Decent housing and respect for the elderly and the opportunity to work — these should be everyone's right."

Senator Kennedy backed up his talk with actions. He helped make the law that allowed 18-year-olds to vote. He visited foreign countries. He advocated a national health care program that would provide medical care to all people, not just those who can afford to pay for it.

And the people continued to show their support of him. He was reelected to the Senate in 1970. He had to remove his name from the list of likely Presidential candidates in both 1972 and 1976. He did not feel the time was right then. He wasn't ready, he said.

But he slowly began to change his mind. He saw the office of the President as the best and most powerful place to get his work done. He felt prepared by his experience.

"I've made my own record," he said. "I'm a man of the Senate, and I can be judged on that."

He also wanted to be judged by his actions, and not just because of his family name. "I'm the person who will be judged, not my brothers," he told reporters.

The Senator's family and friends were worried for him. John and Robert Kennedy had worked hard, but were stopped before they could live out their dreams.

The Senator refused to be afraid. He knew what
could happen, but he would not run from it. He
campaigned just like Honey Fitz and the other
Kennedys. He shook hands, made speeches, and
talked with supporters on sidewalks. It wasn't safe, but
it was the only way he knew how to meet the people.

And on November 7, 1979, he let those people
know that the time was right.

Senator Kennedy, 1975.

THE KENNEDY FAMILY

PATRICK JOSEPH KENNEDY and MARY HICKEY

JOHN "HONEY FITZ" FITZGERALD and ROSE

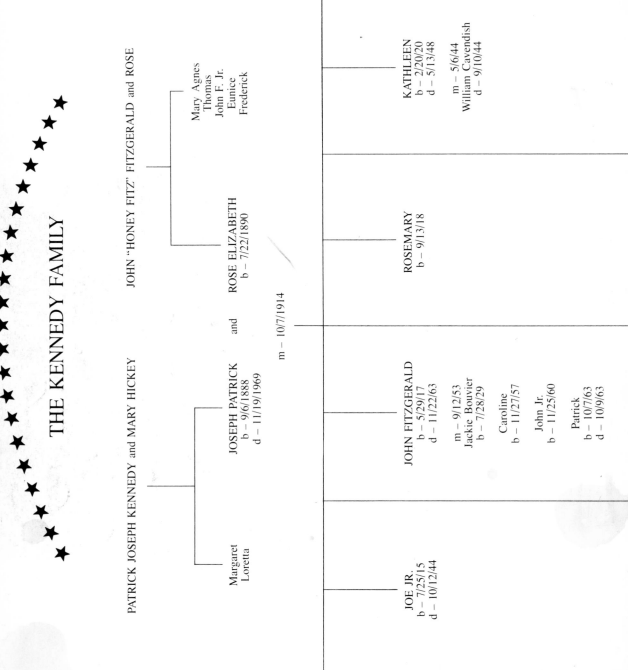

JOSEPH PATRICK
b – 9/6/1888
d – 11/19/1969

Margaret
Loretta

and

ROSE ELIZABETH
b – 7/22/1890

Mary Agnes
Thomas
John F. Jr.
Eunice
Frederick

m – 10/7/1914

JOE JR.
b – 7/25/15
d – 10/12/44

JOHN FITZGERALD
b – 5/29/17
d – 11/22/63

m – 9/12/53
Jackie Bouvier
b – 7/28/29

Caroline
b – 11/27/57

John Jr.
b – 11/25/60

Patrick
b – 10/7/63
d – 10/9/63

ROSEMARY
b – 9/13/18

KATHLEEN
b – 2/20/20
d – 5/13/48

m – 5/6/44
William Cavendish
d – 9/10/44

EUNICE
b – 7/10/21

m – 5/23/53
Sargent Shriver
b – 11/9/15

S. Shriver III
b – 7/28/54

Maria Shriver
b – 11/6/55

Timothy
b – 8/29/59

Mark Kennedy
b – 2/17/64

Anthony Paul
b – 7/20/65

PATRICIA
b – 5/6/24
m – 4/24/54
(Div. 1966)
Peter Lawford
b – 11/7/23

Christopher
b – 3/29/55

Victoria
b – 11/4/58

Sydney
b – 10/25/56

Robin
b – 7/2/61

EDWARD MOORE
b – 2/22/32

m – 11/29/58
Joan Bennett
b – 9/9/36

Kara Anne
b – 2/27/60

Edward Jr.
b – 9/26/61

Partick Joseph
b – 7/14/67

b means "born"
d means "died"
m means "married"

JEAN ANN
b – 2/20/28

m – 5/19/56
Stephen Smith
b – 9/24/27

Stephen
b – 6/28/57

Wm. Kennedy
b – 9/4/60

Amanda Mary
b – 4/30/67
(adopted)

Kym Maria
b – 11/29/72
(adopted)

ROBERT F.
b – 11/20/25
d – 6/6/68

m – 6/16/50
Ethel Skakel
b – 4/11/28

Kathleen
b – 7/4/51

Joe P. III
b – 9/24/52

Robert Jr.
b – 1/17/54

David Anthony
b – 6/15/55

Mary Courtney
b – 9/9/56

David LeMoyne
b – 2/27/58

Mary Kerry
b – 9/8/59

Christopher
b – 7/4/63

Matthew Maxwell
b – 1/1/65

Douglas
b – 3/24/67

Rory Elizabeth
b – 12/12/68

DATE DUE

JAN 30 '87			
MAR 5 '87			
MAR 8 '88			
APR 14 '89			
OCT 5 1992			
FEB 1 6 1999			
MAY 4 2000			
		PRINTED IN U.S.A.	